John & Ann

Wishing you a long &
happy retirement together.

Brenda Downie

Oct '92

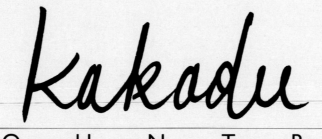

Kakadu

C O U N T R Y

P H O T O G R A P H Y   A N D   T E X T   B Y   P E T E R   J A R V E R

THUNDERHEAD PUBLISHING

DARWIN, AUSTRALIA

C O N T E N T S

I was recently taken to a cave in Kakadu National Park. It was quite near a major tourist access road and because Park staff wanted it left largely unvisited, it was unfenced and unmarked. It was here that archaeologists established that Aboriginal people have been in continuous occupation for over 25,000 years; so long that the coast, then, was three hundred kilometres further north than it is now, the climate cooler and the vegetation much closer to the mulga eucalypt areas still common further south.

Rock art there and nearby showed transition from the earliest styles to depictions of feral pigs and donkeys, and men on horses. That the cave continues to be used was evident from a baking powder tin on a ledge inside. I could only marvel at such a massive history and I delighted at the thought that the descendants of those first cave dwellers now own the Park and are actively involved in its management.

Kakadu is truly a World Park, a place where the rich cultural history of Aboriginal man interlocks with one of the earth's truly great tropic wetland ecosystems. The wildlife, especially the birds, is found in a proliferation rarely matched elsewhere on earth. These assets combined make it easy to understand why UNESCO was so keen to ascribe Stages I and II to the World Heritage list.

James Thorsell of the International Union for Conservation of Nature, the assessor for the World Heritage Committee, has described the listing as "the Nobel prize of national parks."

How lucky we are as a nation to have taken on the role of trustee of some of the best natural assets on Earth, for the benefit not only of Australians, but of all the people of our planet.

Kakadu, Uluru, the Great Barrier Reef, Lord Howe Island, Willandra Lakes, the South West of Tasmania and the New South Wales Rainforests have all been listed. The North Queensland Rainforests will join them in December 1988 and several other places, such as Shark Bay and the Bungle Bungles in Western Australia will surely follow.

But not every place of value will meet the exacting standards of the World Heritage process. It is not even desirable that each should be compared. Certainly there is every reason to cherish all outstanding places, especially those designated national parks, national estate properties, or given some special recognition for their excellence. It is becoming increasingly obvious to the people of Australia that this vast land has become rapidly modified and usually degraded in the two hundred years since colonisation. We do not have infinite supplies of forests, wetlands and arid range lands to exploit. We are realising more and more the value of maintaining a full suit of native flora and fauna species and substantial representations of major ecosystems. We now understand that habitat destruction is overwhelmingly the most common cause for the extinguishing or endangering of species.

The human need for wild places is also becoming better understood. The urbanisation of our lifestyles and the "taming" of the bush has left an emotional void. Few who have walked in wilderness, unmodified by the works of man, would deny the deep spiritual recreation one experiences.

But these places are harder and harder to find. My fifteen years of travelling over most of the southern and western deserts of Australia have convinced me that few truly wild places remain. Petroleum seismic lines, cattle roads and mining roads now criss-cross areas whose Aboriginal owners must have justifiably believed would remain remote and intact forever. But even though the need for our National Parks is great, Kakadu, Katherine Gorge, Gurig and Litchfield Parks will remain under enormous pressure from those who would exploit them commercially–primarily the mining and tourist industries.

Their argument, enshrined in the National Conservation Strategy, is that National Parks, like other areas, should be available for "multiple land use," which allows the co-existence of wilderness use, mining operations, scenic flights, tourist boat rides and accommodation in some equitable or reasonable balance.

The view of the Australian Conservation Foundation is that there is no place for miners and their activities within National Parks. In 1985 only 4.3% of Australia was protected under National Park or some other conservation status. The mining industry has access to the vast bulk of the continent's surface. We have no difficulty in rejecting the industry's right to "share" all parts of the land including Parks.

Kakadu and to a lesser extent, Gurig, are at the centre of this critical debate. Ranger uranium mine already exists in the heart of Kakadu. The miners are seeking to open new uranium mines at Jabiluka and Koongarra and a gold mine at Coronation Hill. They are calling for a mineral exploration area covering the entire catchment area of the South Alligator River, and part of the Katherine and Mary Rivers. The environmental integrity of both the World Heritage wetlands of Kakadu and the Katherine Gorge are at risk. The Foundation will resist any such industrial activity in these and other National Parks in Australia.

Tourism is not so easily dismissed. There is a place for sensitive, low impact tourist activity in Parks, which after all, are for the enjoyment and recreation of visitors. The test to be applied must be–does the tourist proposal significantly degrade the natural values of the Park and visitor enjoyment of those values? If so, the planning mechanism should disallow them. A quiet slow boat ride to watch wildlife may be perfectly compatible, whereas the use of noisy scenic flights, especially by helicopter, may be rejected as being disruptive to both wildlife and to people seeking solitude on the ground. There is no easy solution and each proposal is assessed on its merit.

The great benefit of Peter Jarver's magnificent book is that, through its stunning photographs, many who have not visited the Top End will appreciate how superb it is, and what is at stake when decisions are made regarding its use.

Looking again at the images brings rushing back to me the sights and sounds I experienced during my visit there. It reminds me what a huge responsibility we have to guarantee our descendants the right to experience the same.

Phillip Toyne,
Director,
Australian Conservation Foundation.

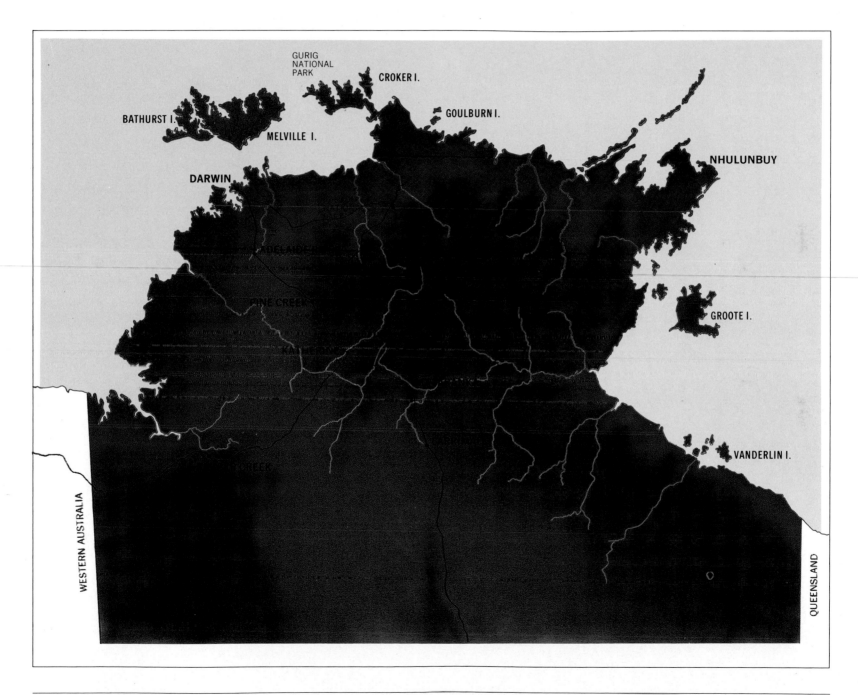

GURIG
NATIONAL
PARK

CROKER I.

GOULBURN I.

BATHURST I.

MELVILLE I.

NHULUNBUY

DARWIN

ADELAIDE

PINE CREEK

GROOTE I.

KA

WESTERN AUSTRALIA

CREEK

VANDERLIN I.

QUEENSLAND

Kakadu

C O U N T R Y

One of Australia's most significant National Parks in terms of both size and diversity of geological, biological and cultural value, Kakadu is destined to become a park of international repute. It is primarily a wilderness area of raw, untamed grandeur, a vast landscape encompassing a rich variety of flora and fauna, all of which is dominated by the seasonal cycling of the Wet and the Dry. This marked change in the weather is reflected in a myriad of ways. The Wet Season period of billowing thundering skies, abundant water, luxuriant growth and explosive population increases contrasts vividly with the harshness of blue smoky skies, dry cracked earth, and a dormant and burnt landscape. This cycle has repeated itself over the millenia, forging the shape and form of the land we now know as Kakadu National Park.

But the cultural heritage of this landscape dates back some 40,000 years or more to the arrival of Aborigines from south-east Asia. Their skilled management of the land has endowed them with a bountiful food supply, and secure shelter along the escarpment combined with ample water and a warm climate has ensured the continuity of a simple but comfortable lifestyle over the ages. Their harmony with the land has nurtured a lifestyle rich in spiritual significance, which has its origins in the Dreamtime legends. This lifestyle and spiritual heritage is generously recorded in the thousands of rock art sites which are found scattered amongst the rock overhangs and caves along the length of the escarpment and overlying plateau. The age and significance of their artwork may be appreciated by the fact that at one particular site, the Long-beaked Echidna, an animal which has been extinct for some 18,000 years has been identified. Indeed, with numerous examples of the various styles of rock paintings depicting everything from the local food supply to Dreamtime creatures, and from X-ray style paintings to impressions of the Aboriginals first contact with European settlers, the park houses one of the richest concentrations of superb rock art in the world.

Many more sites are awaiting discovery, especially in the newly proclaimed area of Stage 3 which takes in magnificent escarpment country along the upper reaches of the South Alligator River. This area has been incorporated in a region euphemistically named the Conservation Zone which is, in fact, reserved for mineral exploration. Hence Stage 3 is under threat from mining operations. The threat to the environment of mining so close to the South Alligator River cannot be overstated. A single spillage of any contaminant would have far-reaching consequences, as this river system links in with the vast floodplains of the World Heritage Areas. In addition, Koolpin Gorge and Waterfall Creek are of great scenic value and views from the surrounding escarpment would quickly be marred by any mining activities.

Ironically, the very geological processes that were responsible for the mineralization which so mesmerizes the mining companies, were also the forces that shaped and formed the Kakadu we see today. These forces are still changing the landscape, the most recent environmental addition being the formation only 1,500 years ago of the freshwater billabongs and paperbark swamps which are a feature of the lower Jim Jim, Nourlangie and Magela Creeks. These billabongs, together with the vast floodplains, form the main feature of the lowlands. Bordering the coastal swamps and tidal flats of the coastline on one side, they extend a considerable distance toward the escarpment, where the wide drifting waters give way to the better defined, faster flowing channels of the respective creeks and rivers.

These floodplains are home to the thousands of birds which rely on the annual inundation cycle to provide the vast store of food that sustains them during the dry months of the year. Congregating in dense flocks in the Dry season, many species disperse more widely in the Wet as they follow the abundance of food generated by heavy monsoonal rains. When the flooding cycle begins, aquatic life runs rampant in its newly formed habitats, providing the first stage of the complex food chain. Once severely damaged by feral buffaloes and pigs these sensitive floodplain areas are rapidly regenerating with carpets of water lilies now growing in profusion.

The floodplains are also sanctuary to the saltwater crocodile, whose numbers were once perilously reduced by the over exploitation of their hides. In 1971 legislation was passed which made it illegal to hunt them, thereby ensuring their survival and a steadily increasing population. The sight of these ancient reptiles in their aquatic habitat is one of the highlights of many people's Kakadu experience.

From the low-lying floodplains the landscape begins to elevate slowly, forming well-drained plains which host eucalypt forests and tropical woodlands. The animal life here is also prolific, but not as noticeable since many of the creatures have nocturnal habits. To the south and the east these lowlands gradually give way to undulating low hills which lie at the foot of the dominant escarpment. This imposing natural barrier is the focal point of Kakadu. Winding its way for some 500 kilometres through the park, the often sheer-walled sandstone escarpment towers above the endless plains, affording magnificent views into the distance. Rising from 100 metres in height at the northern end to an imposing 200 metres at its southern extremity, the richly coloured and deeply eroded rock wall contains a wealth of interesting archaeological features and is home to a large variety of animals who use the intricately weathered rock as a safe refuge. The constantly changing nature of the escarpment is created by the variety of vertical cliffs, stepped cliffs, long talus slopes, and the massive boulders that form the isolated outliers. But perhaps the most interesting feature is found at several widely spaced nick points where the major creeks of the plateau plunge over the escarpment as waterfalls. Jim Jim Falls, Twin Falls and Waterfall Creek are the most prominent of these although numerous small creeks create their own picturesque falls during the heavy monsoonal rains. The larger waterfalls have carved out their own gorges in whose protective and moist environment huddle superb pockets of rainforest.

Overlying this magnificent escarpment is the Arnhem Land plateau, which stretches across the eastern Top End, well beyond the boundaries of Kakadu. It is here in this inhospitable country that the headwaters of all the creeks and rivers are found. The ancient sedimentary rocks have been carved and shaped by faulting and jointing, creating a lattice of dissections which is extremely difficult to traverse.

While a sense of the extraordinary nature of Kakadu may be gleaned from this brief description, it cannot compare with the experience of actually being in this ancient and harshly beautiful landscape. Despite the apparent ruggedness of Kakadu it is a surprisingly fragile environment, and great care must be taken to manage the Park carefully. International recognition has given Australia a park of world significance and with a correct philosophy, Kakadu will be preserved for all future generations.

Waterfall Creek tumbles over rocks along the escarpment of Kakadu National Park, Stage 3

White water cascades through a series of waterfalls in Koolpin Gorge, Stage 3 of Kakadu

Eons of water erosion have carved a path through the sandstone escarpment of Koolpin Gorge

Paperbark trees lean over the crystal clear waters of Nourlangie Creek

Early morning light plays on rapids in Koolpin Creek

Large uprooted bamboo clumps reveal the powerful forces of the South Alligator River's annual flood

An approaching thunderstorm sweeps across the floodplain which surrounds Ubirr

Water lilies and paperbark trees fringe the edges of Yellow Waters

Lush green grass sprawls beneath grey skies as the annual flooding of the Magela begins

White lily flowers flourish on the South Alligator floodplain early in the wet season

Wild Ginger plants clump around rocks at the base of Ubirr

Heavy spray drifts down the gorge below Jim Jim Falls

A delicate stream of water descends onto rocks at the base of the escarpment

Rainforest trees display heat affected leaves resulting from dry season bushfires

Livistona palms grow amid a sandstone outcrop on the Arnhem Land Plateau

A rain-swollen Jim Jim Creek plunges 200 metres over the escarpment

A solid bolt of lightning silhouettes trees during a thunderstorm

A wall of flames advances on a thick tangle of spear grass during the annual fire season

The golden light of sunrise breaks through mist-shrouded paperbark trees

A threatening saltwater crocodile at Yellow Waters

The open-mouthed cooling method used by crocodiles reveals the large teeth of a young animal

A submerging crocodile is easily seen beneath the clear water

A saltwater crocodile consumes a barramundi

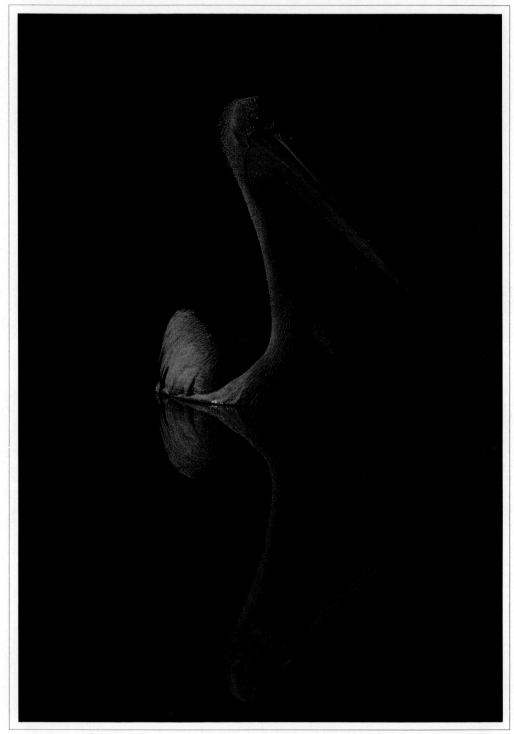

A pelican is mirrored in the late afternoon light of Yellow Waters

Egrets alight in a tree at Yellow Waters

The beautiful Rainbow Bee-eater

A darter bird dries its wings

The night heron is normally found hiding amongst trees

The graceful motion of an egret taking to the air

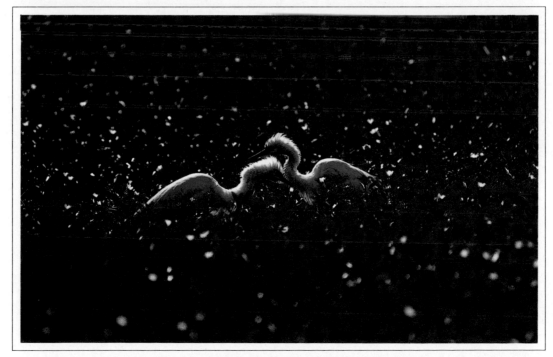

Young egret chicks search for food

top end

L A N D S C A P E S

While Kakadu encompasses many very diverse landforms and can be seen to represent almost every type of Top End landscape, there are three other major Northern Territory parks which have special features of their own.

First and foremost is Katherine Gorge National Park. Established in 1963 it is situated on the southern side of Kakadu, and as such has many features in common with it.

The Gorge itself consists of a chain of chasms and erosion channels carved out of the sandstone rock by the Katherine River, which has its headwaters on the same escarpment plateau as the creeks and rivers of Kakadu. Jim Jim Creek and Twin Falls Creek in fact have adjacent catchment areas and flow northward, while Katherine River flows southward and then to the west, where it flows into the Daly River. As it carves its way through the sandstone, fantastic rock formations and often sheer sided walls form the main features of this perennial water body. Although in an area of lower rainfall, it shares much of the flora and fauna of Kakadu, but due to an absence of floodplains has nowhere near the same profusion of birdlife. In the Wet season it becomes a raging torrent of giant eddies, rapids and whirlpools, and can rise by some 17 metres in height.

While easily accessible by bitumen road and readily viewed by boat tour or canoeing, the upper reaches are for the hardy few, and the Gorge soon becomes a wilderness area visited only by the keen bushwalker or canoeist. A large rockfall between the ninth and tenth gorge effectively blocks canoeing, but walking the escarpment here is not too difficult.

To the west of the Gorge is Edith Falls and more escarpment country. While lacking the overpowering grandeur of the Kakadu escarpment, it is nonetheless magnificent in its own right. Again, many small creeks plunge over the sandstone cliffs and form graceful, intricate little waterfalls surrounded by small pockets of rainforest. Edith Falls is certainly the largest of these and cascades through several sections before entering a large splash-pool, which generates a giant whirlpool action when fed by heavy storm rains. But the Gorge itself is the main attraction of this National Park and is certainly equal in grandeur to any of Kakadu's main geological landforms.

To the north of Kakadu is the Cobourg Peninsula, which in 1981 was declared Gurig National Park and Cobourg Marine Park. The site of one of the first attempts to colonize the Top End, Cobourg Peninsula juts out from the north coast forming the most northerly part of the mainland Northern Territory. This area is an intricate pattern of cays, large bays, tidal flats and mangrove-lined creeks and is renowned for its rich marine life and oyster covered rocks. One of Cobourg's larger bays is the site of a pearl farm which utilizes culturing techniques. However it is the calm sheltered waters, the pristine white sand beaches and startling red rock strata of the peninsula's cliffs which form the main impressions of this remote wilderness area. Accessible by road only through Arnhem Land, the first unusual features of this area to greet the traveller are the large colonies of elegant Kentia palms. Splendid stands of these palms are found right to the water's edge, intermingling with eucalypt forest, casuarina pines and pandanus. Together they give the sweeping bays and burning cliffs a haunting quality of their own. While not a dominating landscape, the subtleties of form, shape and colour have a powerful presence which cannot be denied.

Winding creeks twist their way through dense mangrove-populated tidal flats which ooze the permeating smell of black mud, and click endlessly with the nervous activity of crabs, shells and fish. A true marine jungle, schools of fish are abundant, oysters cling tenaciously to sun-baked rocks and mud-tainted mangrove roots, and dolphins may swim alongside your boat. But the obvious presence of sharks, stingrays and crocodiles reminds the wilderness traveller that the best place to observe this remote tranquillity is from the boat. The numerous white sand beaches are often lined with casuarinas and may be the resting place of some magnificent shells.

Gurig National Park together with Kakadu and Katherine Gorge National Park form an area of some 24,000 square kilometres and incorporate the best of the Top End's ruggedly beautiful landscape. Their National Park status and especially Kakadu's World Heritage status protects these areas from environmental damage of the worst kind, and if managed properly and treated respectfully by the people who visit them, assures a precious gift for all future generations.

Litchfield Park, although smaller in size than the other major parks is also worthy of inclusion. Situated some 120 road kilometres from Darwin, it consists of a smaller escarpment area, but contains several spectacular waterfalls. Here the watercourses tend to be spring-fed, but swollen by wet season rains, can quickly develop into torrents. The crystal-clear waters and sandy-bottomed creeks give welcome respite from the heat, and the area contains some of the biggest stands of Carpentaria palms in the Top End. Clustering together in dense forests, some of these graceful palms curve their way to heights of thirty metres. The flora and fauna are again similar to those of the other parks, with the exception of some rare bats which reside in the escarpment caves and form the only major colonies known to exist. Another feature of this area is the towering magnetic anthills which can reach heights of up to four metres. One of the most impressive colonies of these unusual anthills is to be found just outside the park boundary. It is unfortunate that they were not included in the original park proposal. Covering an area of some two square kilometres, the anthills form the only feature on this essentially treeless blacksoil floodplain, aligning themselves with the earth's magnetic field. The anthills are perhaps a metre wide by only three hundred millimetres thick and taper to a distinct edge on each of two sides. Containing many hundreds of stately peaks made by the small ants from the underlying blacksoil, the area has the appearance of a huge graveyard.

While not presently of National Park status, Litchfield Park should perhaps be designated as such, and careful management plans implemented to protect it from heavy use. Tantalizingly close to Darwin, the park will receive many visitors in a few years time, and special consideration will have to be given to the fragile ecosystems which are unique to Litchfield.

Supplementing the World Heritage area of Kakadu, the importance of Litchfield Park, Katherine Gorge National Park and Gurig National Park cannot be overstated. While the Top End landscape is ruggedly beautiful it is also surprisingly fragile, and climatic variations of the Wet and the Dry place added strain on this environment. Together with elimination of feral buffalo and cattle, the National Park status will do a lot to protect this unique landscape. The following photographs are from a small part of these large parks, and are intended to give the viewer a feel for the intriguing and unusual landscapes of the Top End.

The sheer walls of Katherine Gorge wind their way upstream from Smitt Rock

Rising wet season waters from Edith River inundate a stand of pandanus palms

Edith River races through a set of rapids in Katherine Gorge National Park

Dark storm clouds brewing behind the escarpment highlight lush green spear grass

Thick rainforest provides a canopy of shade over Tolmer Creek, Litchfield Park

Dense rainforest follows the course of Tolmer Creek

Keegan Falls tumbles over the escarpment north of Edith River

Carpentaria palms form the main feature of the rainforest which surrounds the clear waters of Tolmer Creek

Tolmer Falls spills over the escarpment beside a large cave which houses a warm water spring and bat colony

The still waters of Katherine Gorge mirror the colours of sunrise

Water coloured by escarpment reflections tumbles over rocks in Katherine Gorge

A large rockfall marks the tenth gorge on the Katherine River

Smitt Rock, an island of sandstone, lies defiantly in the middle of Katherine Gorge

Litchfield Park, south of Darwin, is home to many spring-fed creeks

Pandanus palms colonize a rocky outcrop on the edge of the plunge pool at Tolmer Falls

The massive root system of an uprooted mangrove tree lies sun-bleached on the sands of Cobourg Peninsula in Gurig National Park

Salt-water intrusion is the likely cause of this graveyard of paperbark trees in Gurig National Park

A thick stand of pandanus on Cobourg Peninsula scatters a carpet of spiky leaves

Numerous magnetic anthills tower skyward near Litchfield Park

Late afternoon sunlight colours the cliffs of Cobourg Peninsula fiery red

Eucalypt forests extend to the calm waters of Cobourg Marine Park

A tidal creek forges a channel through extensive mangrove forests, Gurig National Park

Two meandering creeks unite on the mangrove-populated mudflats of Gurig National Park

top end

CHANGES

The Top End of the Northern Territory is a land of changes and extremes. Driven by the alternating weather patterns of the Wet and the Dry, many distinct and pronounced environmental variations occur, which in turn affect the lifestyle of its people, the viability of agriculture and mining, and the accessibility of its landscape.

Other significant developments have occurred over a longer time span. The original settlers of the Top End were Aboriginal people, who have inhabited the area for perhaps some 40,000 years. Their first outside contact came from Macassan fishermen, who were seasonal visitors interested in procuring and preserving trepang, a marine delicacy. Their presence was established for some 300 years before the arrival of European settlers in 1824.

Difficult economic and physical conditions caused the European community to look for cheaper sources of labour, a quest which resulted in the first influx of Chinese people from Singapore in 1874.

Today, Darwin is home to some forty-five nationalities, the latest additions being the Vietnamese and Timorese refugees who fled their countries in the late 1970's. Along with substantial Greek, German and Italian populations, the influence of the Asian community has been considerable. The change in culinary habits has been especially dramatic, with Asian food stalls in Darwin's numerous markets providing the focus of attention for many a famished browser. The cosmopolitan atmosphere of Darwin has become very pronounced as people of all racial origins interact freely and amicably.

The input from this variety of people has seen Darwin grow from a wood and corrugated iron shanty town to the steel and concrete city that it is today. The people who settled the Top End in years gone by could not possibly have conceived that the capital of the north would one day be a bustling, sports-oriented city, for indeed their own life was far more concerned with survival than deciding in which leisure activity to indulge.

Their difficult past was shaped in more ways than one by that same factor which is today still treated with considerable respect–the weather. The changes wrought are the result of the dramatic climatic cycling between the Dry season and the Wet season. For some five months of the year clear skies assure the suitability of every day to whatever activity one might desire. In fact the only relief from a relentless blue sky is provided by smoke drifting from one of the many bushfires which regularly burn large tracts of the Top End during this season. Smoke from the yellow, dried speargrass softens the piercing blue and creates a haze that sometimes obscures even familiar views.

City-bound Darwinites are desperately keen for weekends of fishing, sailing and visiting their favourite four-wheel drive bush retreats. The parched earth, desperate for rain, subsides into a state of virtual hibernation, reserving its energy for when the rains return once more.

The arrival of the Wet is heralded with a bang–the booming resonance of numerous lightning strikes. The once blue skies become increasingly filled with larger and larger clouds until the dominant colour is the grey of thunderstorms and monsoonal rain. The thirsty earth at first soaks up all that is given, to provide the fuel for an explosion of green. The flattened or burnt speargrass pops out green shoots at an incredible rate and they reach skyward in a frenzy of growth. By the end of the Wet a car could be easily concealed by the three metre high forest of green. But all vehicles are confined to the bitumen now, for the dusty dirt road once used for weekend retreats is all but mud and slush. Dry creek beds once again course water, joining into flows of ever-increasing volume until one major river becomes the sole conveyor of a huge torrent of swirling, muddied water.

The ever-present threat of cyclones is in the back of everyone's mind, but the statistics confirm that this severest of nature's creations rampages through the Top End at only infrequent intervals. Besides the obvious danger of extreme winds is the other major destructive mechanism of the tidal surge. With the normally placid waters heaped upon themselves by the furious wind and swelled by the drop in atmospheric pressure, the added factor of a high tide can spell disaster. Darwin's tidal variation can be as great as eight metres, but fortunately for its inhabitants, the water was at a reasonable level during Cyclone Tracy.

Tidal extremes can also present problems at the other end of the scale. During November 1986 the harbour actually registered a minus tide, presumably indicating that an incorrect zero level was established somewhere back in history. The amount of water drained from Darwin Harbour and Fannie Bay was unbelievable. Land-yachts might have been preferable as the water retreated from the home of Darwin's sailing fleet, creating a situation where people could actually walk out to where the boats were normally anchored. In Francis Bay a narrow channel was all that remained, revealing a vast expanse of mudflats dotted with yachts that leaned almost horizontally.

The Top End is now home to a substantial population of diverse cultural origins. The tide of time has erased past memories, and life in a region of constant change, of extremes of weather, seasons and colours has become the norm. For the visitor or the newly-arrived these fluctuations are impressive, almost bewildering. The senses and emotions are constantly stimulated, the heat and humidity becoming at times, overbearing. But the promise of winters without cold, a great variety of outdoor leisure activities, and with economic opportunities abounding, a great many more people will call Australia's Top End their home.

A dark storm-front is about to deluge the northern suburbs of Darwin

An old Commonwealth Bank agency on Goulburn Island

The new Sheraton Hotel adds to the changing character of Darwin

Intense colours are reflected by the calm waters of Fannie Bay, home of Darwin's sailing fleet

The lowest tide in decades drains Francis Bay of water leaving only the narrow channel of Sadgroves Creek

Casuarina Beach produces a rare display of surf

Casuarina Beach feels the fury of Cyclone Kay

Katherine River bridge easily spans the river during the dry season

Swollen by wet season rains the Katherine River has risen 17 metres

Battered and broken trees lie along Rapid Creek after Cyclone Tracy devastated the area

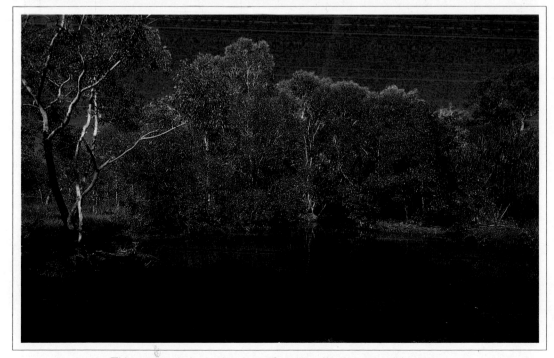

Thirteen years later the signs of cyclone damage are all but gone

Green stands of pandanus contrast starkly with burnt out areas of Holmes Jungle, Darwin

One of the many dry season fires which burn through the Top End each year

Halley's Comet as seen from the Top End

Katherine Gorge is warmed by the colours of moonlight and topped by a myriad of star trails

Victoria Highway, west of Katherine, is the resting place of many a potential hamburger

Francis Bay, Darwin, is the resting place of many deceased vehicles being used as landfill

Spear grass bends with the monsoonal winds of the wet season

A picturesque display of water lilies beside the Stuart Highway near Adelaide River

An alluvial fan feeds a mangrove-lined creek along the west coast of the Top End

Tidal mudflats drain into mangroves near the Adelaide River mouth, on the north coast of the Top End

Pandanus palms contrast starkly with the evening sky and the baked earth of Nightcliff, Darwin

The last rays of sun punctuate the blue of an overcast sky above Nightcliff

The yellow light of sunset filters through a rain shower along Nightcliff Beach

Grey seas swirl around mangroves at Nightcliff as a squall line approaches

sky
SCAPES

The sky presents an eternally unfolding spectacle to the people who live beneath the thin layer of gases, liquids and particles we call the atmosphere. Since time began people have observed in awe, fear and amazement the majestic displays which continually manifest this ocean of air. There are numerous phenomena which are familiar to us all, and a few which still retain their mystery despite the scrutiny of meteorologists who attempt to provide explanations to enhance our familiarity and understanding.

Even though familiar, such commonplace occurrences as sunsets may still have the power to impress and bedazzle, with a riot of colour sweeping across an ethereal surface a surface defined only by the presence of water vapour. It is this physical manifestation of the water contained in the air that defines the broad concept of clouds, and what enormously diverse and varied forms these sailing boats of the skies can assume. Perhaps all too often we take such little notice that when our attention does focus on the skies, the supposedly familiar becomes much less so, as we begin to perceive movements and motions that we had not observed before.

The energies that are responsible for the development of the clouds are largely unseen, and apart from the wind which manifests itself in such familiar ways as the rustling of leaves on a tree, and the sun which can be felt warming the land and the air, the mysterious on-going processes are totally invisible and can be understood and appreciated only when their end product the clouds, have some direct influence on our daily lives.

Their influence is enormous, for in the absence of clouds, we assume the weather to be fine and hence are able to plan any outdoor activities that we wish, but when threatened by rain we must modify or alter that plan, and indeed, if it is actually raining then perhaps it is best to cancel that plan altogether. But the perception of how rain affects our lives is relative. Certainly for people living in the temperate latitudes, rain is generally cool and often accompanied by cold weather, but for a very large number of people who live in the tropics, rain is often the end product of thunderstorms which are generated in conditions of heat and high humidity. The perception then is of welcome relief, for the relatively warm rain is accompanied by cooling breezes and provides a pleasant respite from the oppressive heat.

The Top End of the Northern Territory has much in common with many other tropical areas which have a monsoonal climate. It is not the idyllic tropical island climate of cooling breezes and consistent rainfall which generates that typical lush tropical look. Indeed, for some six months of the year, there is no rain at all. Blue cloudless skies allow the sun to bake the land continuously, punctuated only by hazy, smoky days when distant bushfires fill the air with huge volumes of smoke. For the remainder of the year two different climatic factors control the skies.

The beginning and end of this six month period is dominated by enormous thunderstorms. Some of the largest and most electrically active storms on earth, these clouds pump vast quantities of moist air to the very limits of our weather-producing atmosphere. Driven by the heat of the day, large thermals begin to produce the common cumulus cloud which is familiar to many during the humid times of summer. As these clouds grow in size they band together, allowing updrafts of air to push ever higher. As this process repeats itself, the up-

drafts support more and more water droplets at greater altitudes, giving the base of the cloud an increasingly threatening appearance. At a certain point the weight of rain droplets overcomes the force of the updraft and begins the journey down to the surface. As more and more tumble out of the cloud, the rain becomes heavier and draws a current of air downwards at an ever-increasing rate. This downdraft associated with the rain draws cool air from great altitudes, thus providing the cool winds associated with thunderstorms. During this formation process, the cloud becomes electrically charged and a point is eventually reached when the voltage difference is great enough to stimulate the jagged electrical discharge we all know as lightning.

Because the atmosphere is thicker around the tropical regions of the equator, the troposphere extends to a greater altitude, thereby allowing the thunderstorms to develop on a larger scale. As the enormous thunderheads push skyward, they reach a point in the lower stratosphere where the temperature actually increases, hence counteracting the energy of the updrafts. The rising pillar of cloud has reached the limit of its journey and begins diffusing horizontally, thereby giving the thunderhead its characteristic anvil top.

This process can repeat itself over many hours causing individual thunderstorm cells to develop, mature and decay, and in the process setting the stage for another cell to duplicate this behaviour. The resulting propagation can give the impression that a particular thunderstorm has travelled over a long distance, and indeed, who has not observed in awe, wondrous electrical displays as the thunderstorms dance their way through the night sky. At any given moment some 2,000 thunderstorms are in progress around the world, and during an average day up to 45,000 separate storms are drenching the planet with water, buffeting its occupants with winds and illuminating the skies with fantastic but occasionally lethal displays of lightning.

The Top End receives more than its fair share of energetic thunderstorms, but damage is infrequent and the rains are welcomed. They play a major role in the climate and are familiar to all who live here. The other main weather-producing mechanism of this region is the monsoon, a similar wind system to that which brings life-giving rains to the Asian region. Drawn into northern Australia by the low pressure systems which develop each Wet season, the winds are in fact driven into action by enormous high pressure systems which develop over Siberia each winter. So begins the long journey over thousands of kilometres of tropical seas, gathering moisture as the steady wind traverses the equator. As they converge into low pressure systems over northern Australia, heavy rains may deluge vast areas and promote the vigorous growth of the Wet season that is familiar to those who live here. The rains are widespread and enduring, causing general cloudiness, and bringing welcome relief from the scorching sun.

Welcome though these rains are, the sky lacks the turmoil and visual interest that is generated by the dramatic thunderstorms of the build-up. Possessing shape and form unrivalled anywhere, these electrically charged behemoths traverse the Top End consistently, providing a visual treat which once observed, forever changes one's perception of the sky.

A powerful bolt of lightning strikes the sea just behind Darwin's Supreme Court building

High level cloud streams out from a thunderstorm over the floodplain at Holmes Jungle

Huge thunderheads push upwards assisted by the energy generated from the heat of the day

Heavy storm-clouds sweep low over Darwin as a deluge of rain is about to be released

An afternoon storm discharges a dramatic lightning strike to the sea close to Darwin

An enormous column of cloud rises majestically over Darwin Harbour

A developing thunderstorm cloud obscures the sun during late afternoon

Storm-cloud activity continues against a backdrop of sunset-coloured rain

A line of magpie geese is dwarfed by the billowing clouds of a nearby storm

An intense rainbow stands out vividly against the grey sky

Ice crystals at high altitude refract light into dazzling colours

A night storm over Darwin's northern suburbs is reflected in Rapid Creek

The intense colours of dawn light up an active morning storm

Unusual cloud shapes left by a decayēd thunderstorm

The intense colours of sunset are reflected on Darwin's Fannie Bay

A thunderstorm cell explodes upward over Casuarina Beach, Darwin

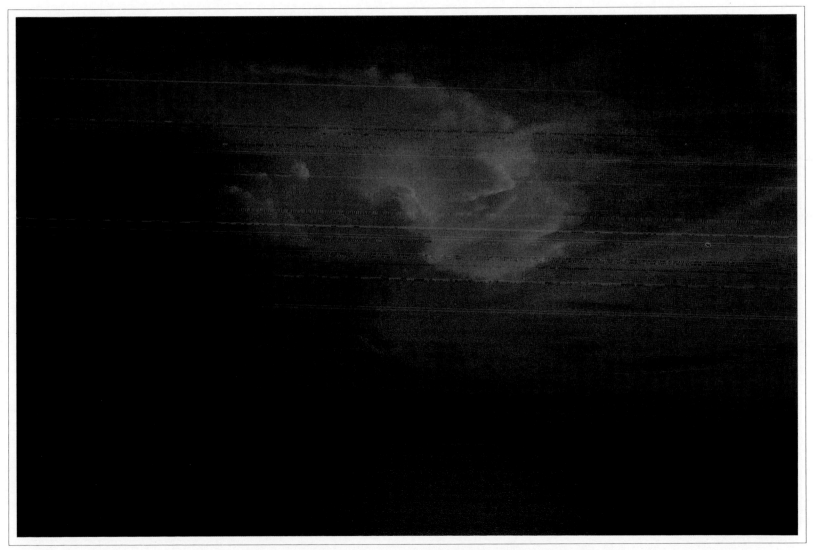

A wide spectrum of colour is reflected from a thunderstorm at sunset

Morning clouds billow over mangroves at Fannie Bay

An afternoon storm develops over unusual rock strata along East Point, Darwin

A thunderstorm billows majestically into the morning sky over Fannie Bay

Two enormous thunderstorms power their way through the evening sky

The sharp edge of a squall line scurries past Nightcliff

Sunrise partially colours a morning storm over Casuarina

A curved squall line passes low over pandanus and spear grass

Sunset colours break through cloud to illuminate a decaying storm

Twin bolts of lightning pierce the night sky over suburban Malak

Lightning streaks horizontally across a rainy sky

Remnant storm-clouds capture the sunset over Nightcliff

Bolts of lightning illuminate the profile of a thunderstorm over Darwin Harbour

Cover	Horseman FA 4 × 5, Schneider 150 mm f5.6
Page 9	Horseman FA 4 × 5, Schneider 90 mm f8, polarizer
Page 10	Horseman FA 4 × 5, Schneider 90 mm f8, polarizer
Page 11	Horseman FA 4 × 5, Schneider 65 mm f5.6, polarizer
Page 12	Horseman FA 4 × 5, Schneider 90 mm f8, polarizer
Page 13	Horseman FA 4 × 5, Schneider 150 mm f5.6
Page 14	Canon F1 35 mm, Canon 28 mm f2, polarizer
Page 15	Canon F1 35 mm, Canon 50 mm f3.5 macro
Page 16	Canon F1 35 mm, Canon 20 mm f2.8, polarizer
Page 17	Nagaoka 4 × 5, Schneider 65 mm f5.6, polarizer
Page 18	Nagaoka 4 × 5, Schneider 90 mm f8, polarizer
Page 19	Nagaoka 4 × 5, Schneider 90 mm f8, polarizer
Page 20	Nagaoka 4 × 5, Schneider 150 mm f5.6, polarizer
Page 21	Nagaoka 4 × 5, Schneider 150 mm f5.6, polarizer
Page 22	Horseman FA 4 × 5, Schneider 150 mm f5.6, polarizer
Page 23	Horseman FA 4 × 5, Schneider 90 mm f8, polarizer
Page 24	Canon F1 35 mm, Canon 20 mm f2.8
Page 25	Canon F1 35 mm, Canon 28 mm f2
Page 26	Canon F1 35 mm, Canon 28 mm f2
Page 27	Canon F1 35 mm, Canon 80-200 mm f4 zoom
Page 28	(Top) Canon F1 35 mm, Canon 300 mm f4L
Page 28	(Bottom) Canon F1 35 mm, Canon 80-200 mm f4 zoom
Page 29	(Top) Rollei 6006, Planar 80 mm f2.8, circular polarizer
Page 29	(Bottom) Canon F1 35 mm, Canon 300 mm f4L
Page 30	Canon F1 35 mm, Canon 80-200 mm f4 zoom
Page 31	(Top) Canon F1 35 mm, Canon 300 mm f4L
Page 31	(Bottom) Canon F1 35 mm, Canon 300 mm f4L
Page 32	(Top) Canon F1 35 mm, Canon 300 mm f4L
Page 32	(Bottom) Canon F1 35 mm, Canon 300 mm f4L
Page 33	(Top) Canon F1 35 mm, Canon 300 mm f4L
Page 33	(Bottom) Canon F1 35 mm, Canon 300 mm f4L
Page 37	Horseman FA 4 × 5, Schneider 150 mm f5.6, polarizer
Page 38	Horseman FA 4 × 5, Schneider 90 mm f8, polarizer
Page 39	Horseman FA 4 × 5, Schneider 90 mm f8, polarizer
Page 40	Horseman FA 4 × 5, Schneider 150 mm f5.6, polarizer
Page 41	Horseman FA 4 × 5, Schneider 90 mm f8, polarizer
Page 42	Horseman FA 4 × 5, Schneider 90 mm f8, polarizer
Page 43	Horseman FA 4 × 5, Schneider 90 mm f8, polarizer
Page 44	Horseman FA 4 × 5, Schneider 90 mm f8, polarizer
Page 45	Horseman FA 4 × 5, Schneider 150 mm f5.6
Page 46	Horseman FA 4 × 5, Schneider 90 mm f8
Page 47	Horseman FA 4 × 5, Schneider 90 mm f8
Page 48	Horseman FA 4 × 5, Schneider 90 mm f8
Page 49	Horseman FA 4 × 5, Schneider 90 mm f8
Page 50	Horseman FA 4 × 5, Schneider 90 mm f8, polarizer
Page 51	Horseman FA 4 × 5, Schneider 90 mm f8, polarizer
Page 52	Canon F1 35 mm, Canon 20 mm f2.8, polarizer
Page 53	Canon F1 35 mm, Canon 28 mm f2, polarizer
Page 54	Horseman FA 4 × 5, Schneider 150 mm, polarizer
Page 55	Horseman FA 4 × 5, Schneider 90 mm, polarizer
Page 56	Canon T70 35 mm, Canon 20 mm f2.8, polarizer
Page 57	Horseman FA 4 × 5, Schneider 150 mm f5.6
Page 58	Canon T70 35 mm, Canon 28 mm f2, polarizer
Page 59	Canon F1 35 mm, Canon 50 mm f3.5 macro, polarizer
Page 63	Nagaoka 4 × 5, Schneider 65 mm f5.6
Page 64	Canon F1 35 mm, Canon 28 mm f2, polarizer
Page 65	Horseman FA 4 × 5, Schneider 65 mm f5.6, polarizer
Page 66	Canon F1 35 mm, Canon 500 mm f4.5L, 2 × converter
Page 67	Canon F1 35 mm, Canon 20 mm f2, polarizer
Page 68	Rollei 6006 6 × 6 cm, Rolleigon 50 mm f4, polarizer
Page 69	Canon F1 35 mm, Canon 300 mm f4L
Page 70	(Top) Canon F1 35 mm, Canon 28 mm f2, polarizer
Page 70	(Bottom) Canon T70 35 mm, Canon 28 mm f2, polarizer
Page 71	(Top) Minolta SRT 101 35 mm. Rokkor 20 mm f2.8, polarizer
Page 71	(Bottom) Canon F1 35 mm, Canon 20 mm f2.8, polarizer
Page 72	Canon F1 35 mm, Canon 300 mm f4L, 2 × converter
Page 73	Canon F1 35 mm, Canon 20 mm f2.8
Page 74	Canon F1 35 mm, Canon 300 mm f4L, equatorial mount
Page 75	Canon T70 35 mm, Canon 20 mm f2.8, command back 70
Page 76	Canon F1 35 mm, Canon 20 mm f2.8, polarizer
Page 77	Rollei 6006 6 × 6 cm, Distagon 40 mm f4
Page 78	Canon F1 35 mm, Canon 28 mm f2
Page 79	Horseman FA 4 × 5, Schneider 90 mm f8, polarizer
Page 80	Canon F1 35 mm, Canon 50 mm f3.5 macro
Page 81	Canon T70 35 mm, Canon 80-200 mm f4 zoom
Page 82	Rollei 6006 6 × 6 cm, Rolleigon 50 mm f4
Page 83	Horseman FA 4 × 5, Schneider 150 mm f5.6
Page 84	Horseman FA 4 × 5, Schneider 150 mm f5.6
Page 85	Horseman FA 4 × 5, Schneider 90 mm f8, polarizer
Page 89	Rollei 6006 6 × 6 cm, Planar 80 mm f2.8, lightning trigger
Page 90	Rollei 6006 6 × 6 cm, Planar 80 mm f2.8
Page 91	Canon F1 35 mm, Canon 28 mm f2
Page 92	Horseman FA 4 × 5, Schneider 65 mm f5.6
Page 93	Canon F1 35 mm, Canon 28 mm f2, lightning trigger
Page 94	Rollei 6006 6 × 6 cm, Planar 80 mm f2.8, 2 × converter, polarizer
Page 95	Horseman FA 4 × 5, Schneider 90 mm f8, polarizer
Page 96	Canon F1 35 mm, Canon 300 mm f4L
Page 97	Canon F1 35 mm, Canon 300 mm f4L
Page 98	Canon F1 35 mm, Canon 300 mm f4L
Page 99	Canon F1 35 mm, Canon 300 mm f4L
Page 100	Rollei 6006 6 × 6 cm, Planar 80 mm f2.8, 2 × converter
Page 101	Rollei 6006 6 × 6 cm, Distagon 40 mm f4
Page 102	Canon F1 35 mm, Canon 28 mm f2
Page 103	Canon F1 35 mm, Canon 20 mm f2.8
Page 104	Canon F1 35 mm, Canon 20 mm f2.8
Page 105	Horseman FA 4 × 5, Schneider 150 mm f5.6
Page 106	Canon F1 35 mm, Canon 28 mm f2, polarizer
Page 107	Canon F1 35 mm, Canon 50 mm f3.5 macro, polarizer
Page 108	Canon F1 35 mm, Canon 50 mm f3.5 macro, polarizer
Page 109	Horseman FA 4 × 5, Schneider 90 mm f8, polarizer
Page 110	Rollei 6006 6 × 6 cm, Distagon 40 mm f4
Page 111	Rollei 6006 6 × 6 cm, Planar 80 mm f2.8
Page 112	Rollei 6006 6 × 6 cm, Distagon 40 mm f4
Page 113	Rollei 6006 6 × 6 cm, Planar 80 mm f2.8
Page 114	Rollei 6006 6 × 6 cm, Rolleigon 50 mm f4
Page 115	Rollei 6006 6 × 6 cm, Planar 80 mm f2.8
Page 116	Horseman FA 4 × 5, Schneider 90 mm f8
Page 117	Horseman FA 4 × 5, Schneider 150 mm f5.6

Films used:
4 × 5 Fujichrome 100, 6 × 6 (120 roll) Fujichrome 100
35 mm Kodachrome 64, 35 mm Kodachrome 200

POSTERS

Available from
"The Top End of Down Under"
and
"Kakadu Country"

Black Lightning 610 × 726 mm

Misty Morning 610 × 726 mm

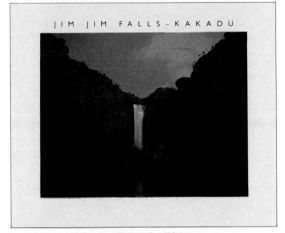

Jim Jim Falls 610 × 726 mm

Sunset Lightning 610 × 726 mm

LIMITED EDITION PRINTS

Original signed Cibachrome prints in
editions of 50 are available in different
sizes.
For more information on posters and
limited edition prints, please write to

THUNDERHEAD PUBLISHING
G.P.O. Box 2914
Darwin N.T. 5794 Australia

OTHER TITLES BY PETER JARVER

"The Top End of
Down Under"

Thunderhead Publishing

First published by Thunderhead Publishing, 1988
1st Reprint 1989
G.P.O. Box 2914 DARWIN N.T. 5794 Australia. Telephone (089) 81 6541

Design by David Doyle-David Hughes Design
Melbourne, Victoria, Australia
Printed in Hong Kong by Dai Nippon
©Peter Jarver 1988

Jarver, Peter, 1953–
Kakadu Country
ISBN 0 9589067 1 8.
1. Northern Territory–Description and travel–1976–Views.
2. Darwin (N.T.)–Description–1976–Views.
3. Kakadu National Park (N.T.)–Description and travel–1976–Views. I. Title.
994.2906'3'0222

Acknowledgements:
Andrew Reynolds for the Top End map
Canon Professional Services for loan of equipment
Phil Burt of Cooinda Four Seasons Motel for boat facilities
Marilyn Venus for editing assistance
Willy Burgess for the dust jacket portrait